W9-CPP-530

鳥 山 明

I don't know how many times I've said it–I hate the cold and I hate winter! I wish I could hibernate like a bear. I often get invited to go skiing, but there's no way I would go. Why would I go out of my way to go someplace that's so cold? But on the other hand, I love it when it's hot, in the summertime! I get so excited! That's why it's mostly summer in my manga. I love the summer! Now if only there weren't any mosquitoes...

–Akira Toriyama, 1989

Artist/writer Akira Toriyama burst onto the manga scene in 1980 with the wildly popular **Dr. Slump**, a science fiction comedy about the adventures of a mad scientist and his android "daughter." In 1984 he created his hit series **Dragon Ball**, which ran until 1995 in Shueisha's best-selling magazine **Weekly Shonen Jump**, and was translated into foreign languages around the world. Since **Dragon Ball**, he has worked on a variety of short series, including **Cowa!**, **Kajika**, **SandLand**, and **Neko Majin**, as well as a children's book, **Toccio the Angel**. He is also known for his design work on video games, particularly the **Dragon Warrior** RPG series. He lives with his family in Japan.

DRAGON BALL Z VOL. 2
SHONEN JUMP Manga Edition

STORY AND ART BY
AKIRA TORIYAMA

English Adaptation/Gerard Jones
Translation/Lillian Olsen
Touch-Up Art & Lettering/Wayne Truman
Cover Design/Izumi Evers & Dan Ziegler
Graphics & Design/Sean Lee
Original Editor/Trish Ledoux
Editor/Jason Thompson

DRAGON BALL © 1984 by BIRD STUDIO. All rights reserved. First published in Japan in 1984 by SHUEISHA Inc., Tokyo. English translation rights arranged by SHUEISHA Inc.

Some nudity has been modified from the original Japanese edition.

The stories, characters, and incidents mentioned in this publication are entirely fictional.

No portion of this book may be reproduced or transmitted in any form or by any means without written permission from the copyright holders.

In the original Japanese edition, DRAGON BALL and DRAGON BALL Z are known collectively as the 42-volume series DRAGON BALL. The English DRAGON BALL Z was originally volumes 17–42 of the Japanese DRAGON BALL.

Printed in the U.S.A.

Published by VIZ Media, LLC
P.O. Box 77010
San Francisco, CA 94107

10
First printing, March 2003
Tenth printing, October 2013

www.viz.com

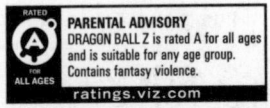

www.shonenjump.com

SHONEN JUMP MANGA

DRAGON BALL Z

Vol. 2

DB: 18 of 42

STORY AND ART BY
AKIRA TORIYAMA

THE MAIN CHARACTERS

Son Gohan
Goku's four-year-old son. As a half-human, half-Saiyan, he may be even stronger than a regular Saiyan!

Son Goku
The greatest martial artist on Earth. Although he looks human, he's actually one of the alien Saiyans. Unlike most Saiyans, he does not have a monkey's tail, as it was cut off several years ago.

Bulma
Goku's oldest friend, Bulma is a scientific genius. She met Goku while on a quest for the seven magical Dragon Balls which, when gathered together, can grant any wish.

Tenshinhan
Three-eyed Tenshinhan is one of Goku's former rivals.

Yamcha
A former bandit and martial artist, Yamcha is Bulma's ex-boyfriend.

Kuririn
Goku's former martial arts schoolmate under Kame-Sen'nin.

Son Goku was Earth's greatest hero, but no one knew where he got his strength…until a stranger came from outer space bearing the news that Goku was an alien! The shocking news turned worse when the stranger, Goku's brother Raditz, proved to be a ruthless killer. By teaming up with his old enemy Piccolo, Goku was able to defeat his extraodinarily powerful brother…only to die in the process. Now, Goku has gone to the afterlife, and Earth is in even more trouble…in one year, Raditz's partners will arrive to steal the Dragon Balls and wipe out all life on Earth!!

Piccolo
Goku's arch-enemy, Piccolo *Daimaô* ("Piccolo the Great Demon King") once tried to become ruler of the world.

Kami-sama
The deity who watches over the Earth, Kami-sama is the good side to Piccolo's evil. He is assisted by Mr. Popo.

Vegeta & Nappa
The two Saiyan warriors who will arrive on Earth in one year.

Kame-Sen'nin
Kame-Sen'nin, also known as the "Turtle Hermit" or *Muten-Rôshi* (the "Invincible Old Master"), helped train Goku and Kuririn in the martial arts.

DRAGON BALL Z 2

Tale 11 A Warrior in Hell 7

Tale 12 Gohan and Piccolo 22

Tale 13 Son Gohan, the Inconsolable 36

Tale 14 Deeds Done by the Full Moon 50

Tale 15 Goku and Gohan's Training Begins!!! 64

Tale 16 Masters and Students 78

Tale 17 The Hardest Time of His Death 92

Tale 18 Closer...Closer... 106

Tale 19 The Day of the Saiyans 120

Tale 20 Let the Games Begin! 134

Tale 21 One Down... 148

Tale 22 Heroes in Terror 162

Title Page Gallery 176

DBZ:11

A Warrior in Hell

BUT IF IT'S THE DIVINE KAMI-SAMA, WE DON'T HAVE TO WORRY? RIGHT? R-RIGHT...?
WH-WHO KNOWS WHAT HE'LL DO...
WHAT...?! KAMI-SAMA TOOK GOKU'S BODY...?!

DIDN'T YOU CHASE HIM AWAY...?
ARRGH! WHERE DID YAMCHA GO, NOW THAT WE NEED HIM ?!

...TO BRING GOKU BACK TO LIFE.
WE'VE JUST GOTTA GATHER THE OTHER SIX DRAGON BALLS...

HUH ?
THE QUEER MACHINE MOUNTED ON HIS FACE SEEMS TO TRACK AN OPPONENT'S STRENGTH AND POSITION...

WAIT A MINNIT... THAT SO-CALLED BROTHER OF GOKU'S...
!?
HOW'D HE FIND HIM SO EASILY...?

*THE "TURTLE" HOUSE...ALSO KNOWN AS THE "KAME" HOUSE!--ED.

NN NGG..!!
PICCOLO... WHAT ARE YOU GOING TO...

:WHEW:
TWIK TWIK

...GGYAAA!!!
ZHOOP

L-LIKE A... LIZARD...
UH...
...

IN THE MEANTIME... I'LL TAKE SON GOKU'S SON.
BE SURE TO FIND THOSE DRAGON BALLS. EVEN KAMI-SAMA LACKS THE POWER TO BRING THE DEAD BACK TO LIFE.

I AM NOT !!!
YOU'RE GONNA EAT HIM !!
--I KNOW !

WH-WHAT ?!
Y-YOU'RE KIDDING! WH-WHAT ARE YOU GONNA...

WE'LL NEED HIS POWER AGAINST THE TWO SAIYANS WHO WILL BE HERE WITHIN THE YEAR...
THAT BOY WILL BE A POWERFUL ASSET... ONCE HE'S TRAINED.
...AND ONLY I CAN TRAIN HIM PROPERLY.

TRY TO STOP ME AND I'LL KILL YOU ALL!
--WE HAVE NO TIME FOR THAT!
W-WE SHOULD ASK GOKU OR HIS MOTHER BEFORE WE...
IT'S KIND OF A BIG RESPONS-IBILITY, RIGHT...?
W-W-WELL YEAH, B-BUT...

HYUUU
B-BUT... BUT...!

D-DO-DON'T LOOK AT ME...!!
...
IF THE KID'S LUCKY... HE'LL ONLY TURN INTO A SUPER-VILLAIN...

TELL SON GOKU TO BE PATIENT... IF HE COMES BACK TO LIFE, THAT IS.
IN ONE YEAR'S TIME, I'LL BRING THE BRAT BACK TO YOU.

THE UNDER-WORLD...
Y'KNOW... GOKU 'N' CHI-CHI ARE GONNA PITCH A FIT OVER THIS--
ALL SOULS, PLEASE REMAIN IN LINE AND CONTINUE MOVING.
WELCOME
NO CUTTING, PLEASE! THANK YOU!
BLAH BLAH
BLAH

*ENMA DAI-Ō, KNOWN IN JAPANESE MYTH AND FOLKLORE AS THE LORD AND JUDGE OF THE DEAD!

SAY, DOES EVERYONE COME HERE WHEN THEY DIE?
EVEN ALIENS ?
YOU'RE HERE, AREN'T YOU? THE DEAD OF ALL WORLDS COME HERE FOR RELOCATION, EITHER TO HEAVEN OR HELL...
THEY DO.

YES, HE DID. YOUR BROTHER, WASN'T HE? STRAIGHT TO HELL, OF COURSE.
WHO'S WHO

HEY, DID A GUY NAMED RADITZ COME HERE A LITTLE WHILE AGO?
EH ?
AK! DON'T SPEAK TO A LORD LIKE THAT!
HEENMA

BEATING THAT GUY...
...NOW THAT'S AWE-SOME!

WHOA... !
INDEED HE DID. BUT NONE DEFEAT ME.
CLOSED

DIDN'T HE FIGHT IT?!

PERHAPS KAMI-SAMA NEEDS A LITTLE RETRAINING IN HELL, HMM?
...I HEARD THAT.
LOWER YOUR VOICE, IDIOT! DON'T LET LORD ENMA HEAR YOU!
KAIÔ-SAMA'S THE STRONGER OF THE TWO ANYWAY.
MAYBE I OUGHTA BE TRAINED BY HIM!!
IF YOU WANT THE LORD OF WORLDS SO BADLY... GO!
IT IS DONE!
YOU NEVER WERE A VERY FUNNY GOD...
...
I-I MEAN... WHAT BIG EARS YOU HAVE... HA HA...
F-F-FORGIVE ME, MY LORD! I DIDN'T THINK YOU'D HEAR...
WAIT FOR THE GUIDE BY THE SIDE ENTRANCE.
TH-TH-THANK YOU, SIR!
PLEASE NOTE MANAGEMENT TAKES NO RESPONSIBILITY FOR WHAT HAPPENS ON THE SERPENT ROAD.
THE LORD ENMA

WELL THEN... GOOD LUCK. YOU'LL NEED IT THIS YEAR.
I'LL TAKE YOUR WORD FOR IT! I'LL TELL KAIŌ-SAMA, THIS "LORD OF WORLDS" GUY, THAT YOU SENT ME!
SAY HI TO MR. POPO FOR ME, HUH?

THIS TIME, WE MAY NOT COME THROUGH SO EASILY...
WHAT A FINE MESS THE EARTH HAS GOTTEN ITSELF INTO...

WILL YOU QUIT THINKING SO LOUD !?
SHUT UP !!!
YOW !!!
THE HON. ENMA

SON GOKU MAY BE TRAINED BY THE LORD OF WORLDS, BUT WE CANNOT KNOW HOW MUCH STRONGER HE CAN BECOME...
TRUE, WE MAY WELL ASK SHENLONG FOR THE OBLITERATION OF THE SAIYANS, BUT EVEN HIS POWER MAY NOT BE ENOUGH...
OUR ONLY HOPE MAY BE SON GOKU'S SON... AND HOW DO WE KNOW WHAT PICCOLO WILL RAISE HIM TO BE...?
MMBLE...
MTTER...

ASIDE FROM BEING DEAD, YOU MEAN...?
PUTT PUTT PUTT
SORRY TO KEEP YOU WAITING! I'LL BE YOUR GUIDE TO THE HEAD OF THE SERPENT. IT'S QUITE A TRIP! ARE YOU IN GOOD HEALTH?

HERE WE ARE!
BINGO!

WHO, KAIŌ-SAMA? THE LORD OF WORLDS STANDS ABOVE ALL THE GODS OF THE UNIVERSE!
...SAY, WHAT'S THIS "LORD OF WORLDS" LIKE?

FOLLOW THE GREEN SCALE ROAD! IT'LL LEAD YOU STRAIGHT TO THE LORD HIMSELF!
Y-YOU MEAN THE "SERPENT ROAD" IS REALLY A SERPENT?! N-NOW WHAT?!

H-HOW LONG IS IT...?
THE LEGEND SAYS IT'S ABOUT A MILLION KILOMETERS.

AND... N-NOBODY ELSE...?
WELL...IF ONE GUY CAN DO IT...TWO GUYS CAN DO IT...

ABSOLUTELY! LORD ENMA'S DONE IT! AND IN JUST THE PAST HUNDRED MILLION YEARS!

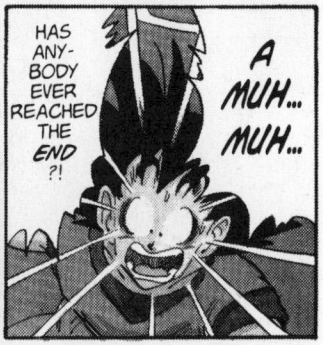
HAS ANY-BODY EVER REACHED THE *END* ?!
A MUH... MUH...

YOU'LL BE FINE, SIR! YOU'RE ALREADY DEAD, SO YOU CERTAINLY CAN'T STARVE TO DEATH!
GEEZ... I DIDN'T EVEN BRING A LUNCH...
OH YEAH...

HELL'S RIGHT DOWN THERE, AND YOU'LL NEVER GET OUT.
BE CAREFUL NOT TO FALL OFF INTO THE CLOUDS.
R-RIGHT...

*A.K.A. "BABA URANAI," A WISE, WIZENED CRONE (LIKE BABA YAGA!) FIRST MET BY GOKU & CO. IN EARLIER ***DRAGON BALL*** STORIES.

NEXT: A STERN TASKMASTER

HYNNNNN

TIME TO WAKE UP, CHILD OF MINE.

PLASH

BURBLE URBLE
BLOOSH
FEH!
KOFF KOFF
HUHH !
HUH ?!
WE HAVE TO TALK. GET OUT OF THE WATER.
!?
huff huff

WH-WHO ARE YOU...?!
EEK!

BLASH BLASH
DAAA-DDY!!!
WHERE ARE YOU?!
HELP MEEEEE!!!

WH-WHERE'S DADDY...?!
!!!

BLASH BLASH
...MORE THAN ENOUGH TROUBLE!
AAA!!!
EEK!!!

I THINK YOU'VE GIVEN ME...
MY BOY...

DAD-DYYYY! WAAAAH!!!
I'M SCARED!!!

OR I'LL SLIT YOUR THROAT !!!
SILENCE!!!!

WAAAAH !!!
WAAAAH !!!

HE GAVE HIS LIFE TO SAVE YOU FROM THAT KIDNAPPER !
YOUR FATHER IS DEAD !

NOW LISTEN TO ME...
sniff
sniff
sniff

DON'T EVEN START, BOY!
sniff
sniff

D...
DAD-D-D-DY...

!!

WE DEFEATED YOUR KIDNAPPER... BUT TWO OTHERS EVEN MORE POWERFUL THAN HE ARE ON THEIR WAY HERE.
HIS DEATH IS NOT THE PROBLEM.
YOU'VE HEARD ABOUT THE DRAGON BALLS, HAVEN'T YOU? GOKU'S FRIENDS WILL GATHER THEM AND HE WILL EVENTUALLY BE BROUGHT BACK TO LIFE.

WE NEED YOUR POWER!! YOU MUST LEARN TO USE THAT POWER--AND JOIN US IN PROTECTING THE EARTH!!!
EVEN WHEN GOKU COMES BACK TO LIFE, HE AND I ALONE WILL HAVE NO CHANCE!!

THE TRAINING OF PICCOLO WILL BRING IT OUT!
YOU HAVE POWER HIDDEN WITHIN YOU THAT YOU HAVE NEVER EVEN GLIMPSED!

B-B-BUT I C-CAN'T FIGHT...I CAN'T!!
WHAT...?! MUH-MUH-MUH-ME?!

DO YOU WANT PROOF ?

I...I DON'T HAVE ANY POWER...
Y-YOU'RE LYING...

WHAT ARE YOU DOING ?!
OWWW !!

GOMP
NO !! STOP !!

EEEEEK !!!

AAAA!!!
YAA!!
EEE-YAA!!
WAAA!!!

...OR TURN TO JELLY AGAINST THOSE ROCKS!!
FIND THE POWER QUICKLY, BOY...
AARH

VMMM
GWOM

!!
DOOM
ズズ

HYUUUUUU...

!!

THAT'S... MORE THAN I IMAGINED...

...

D-DID I...DO THAT...?!
IT BEGINS TO COME CLEAR, DOESN'T IT, BOY?

REARING THE CUB WHO MAY SOMEDAY BECOME MY MOST FORMIDABLE FOE...?
WHAT AM I IN FOR...?

YOUR POWER BURSTS LOOSE ONLY WHEN YOUR EMOTIONS ARE AT THEIR PEAK...
...AND THEN ONLY FOR AN INSTANT. NOT VERY USEFUL...
BUT I WILL TEACH YOU HOW TO USE THAT POWER ALL THE TIME. I WILL MAKE YOU THE GREATEST FIGHTER EVER!

BE WHAT-EVER YOU WANT, INFANT... *AFTER* YOU'VE DEFEATED THE TWO SAIYANS WHO WILL BE HERE NEXT YEAR.
IF YOU FAIL, THEY'LL EXTERMINATE EVERYONE ON EARTH. THAT WOULD PUT A CRIMP INTO YOUR CAREER PLANS, EH?

BUT... BUT I...
...I DON'T WANT TO BE A FIGHTER... I WANT TO BE A GREAT SCHOLAR...

QUIT WHINING!!! OR I'LL KILL YOU RIGHT *NOW*!!!
DISCUSSION TIME IS *OVER*!!! TAKE OFF YOUR SURCOAT!!!

B-BUT I'M...I'M SCARED..

NEXT: MISERY LOVES COMPANY

WH-WHAT DO I DO... F-FOR TRAINING...?

SURVIVE HERE, ALONE.
THAT'S RIGHT.
WHAT...?! L-LIVE...?!

LIVE.
FIRST, DO NOTHING.

I-I DON'T WANT TO, I-I'LL DIE OF LONELI-NESS!!
A-ALONE FOR SIX MONTHS AT A PLACE LIKE THIS...?!

I'LL TEACH YOU HOW TO FIGHT.
IF YOU'RE STILL ALIVE WHEN I COME BACK IN SIX MONTHS...

SURVIVE FOR SIX MONTHS SOMEHOW, AND LEARN HOW TO BE TOUGH.
LISTEN! YOU HAVE NO TIME FOR THIS INFANTILE BEHAVIOR!
MENTALLY AND PHYSICALLY!

HEH HEH...YOU WON'T BE ALONE. THIS PLACE IS SWARMING WITH BLOOD-THIRSTY BEASTS.
WH-WHAT?! D-DON'T, PLEASE DON'T LEAVE ME!!

DON'T FORGET THAT YOU HOLD THE KEY TO THE EARTH'S FATE.
BELIEVE IN YOUR POWER. AND FIGURE OUT BY YOURSELF HOW TO EFFECTIVELY DRAW OUT THAT POWER.
B-BUT BUT I...!

A WORLD OF DEATH THAT MAKES THIS PLACE LOOK LIKE A PARADISE...
...OH, AND BY THE WAY? DON'T EVEN THINK ABOUT ESCAPING. THIS PLACE IS SURROUNDED BY DESERT...
SEE YA.

POOR LITTLE PRINCE-LING...
DO YOU THINK THOSE THINGS ARE PREPARED FOR YOU?

WHERE DO I GET FOOD?!
W-WAIT!
AND A BATH?! AND A BED?!

IF YOU WANT TO FEEL RESENTMENT, CURSE YOUR OWN FATE... AS DO I.

...
B-BUT... THAT'S NOT FAIR...

VOO
AH !!!
WAAH !
WAAAIT !!!
I'M SCAAARED !!! DON'T LEAVE MEEE!

...

YOU SEEM TROUBLED, MY LORD...
WHAT IS THE MATTER ?
神

THAT WAS MY THOUGHT AS WELL... ONE THING IS CERTAIN: NO LONGER IS HE THE "DAI-MAÔ" OF OLD.
HE IS DEFINITELY EVIL, BUT IT FEELS LIKE THE CRUDE, CUNNING VIOLENCE HE ONCE HAD IS GONE...
OUR PICCOLO... IT SEEMS THAT HE IS INDEED DIFFERENT FROM BEFORE...

PERHAPS HE IS EVEN AWARE OF IT...
...AWARE THAT I...AND THUS HE, PICCOLO... HAVE ONLY ONE YEAR TO LIVE...

USUALLY, THE SOULS OF THOSE KILLED BY DEMONS CANNOT REST IN PEACE, AND DRIFT IN SPACE, SUFFERING... THE FACT THAT THE PICCOLO-KILLED RADITZ WAS IN THE UNDER-WORLD, NEVERTHELESS, MEANS THAT PICCOLO IS CLEARLY DIFFERENT FROM BEFORE...
I KNEW THAT THERE WAS SOME-THING AMISS WHEN RADITZ'S SOUL, AFTER HE WAS KILLED BY PICCOLO, ENDED UP IN THE UNDER-WORLD...

...OR IF MY LIFE SPAN HAPPENS TO END AT THAT TIME...
I DO NOT KNOW, HOW-EVER, IF THAT IS BECAUSE PICCOLO IS GOING TO BE KILLED BY THE SAIYANS WHEN THEY ARRIVE IN A YEAR...
神

ONE YEAR...
...

HE MIGHT BE WANTING TO LEAVE SOMETHING BEHIND...EVEN IF IT IS IN SON GOKU'S SON...
HE KNOWS THIS...
神

MY DEATH IS PICCOLO'S DEATH, AND PICCOLO'S DEATH IS MY DEATH...
HEH HEH... IT IS NOT A PLEASANT THING, EVEN AS A GOD, TO KNOW ONE'S OWN DEATH...

YES...THE NEXT TIME THEY ARE USED WILL BE THEIR LAST...
THEN THE DRAGON BALLS...

IM SCAAARED...
WEHH...
sob sob...

!!

BOOM
SNIFF...

BOOM
BOOM

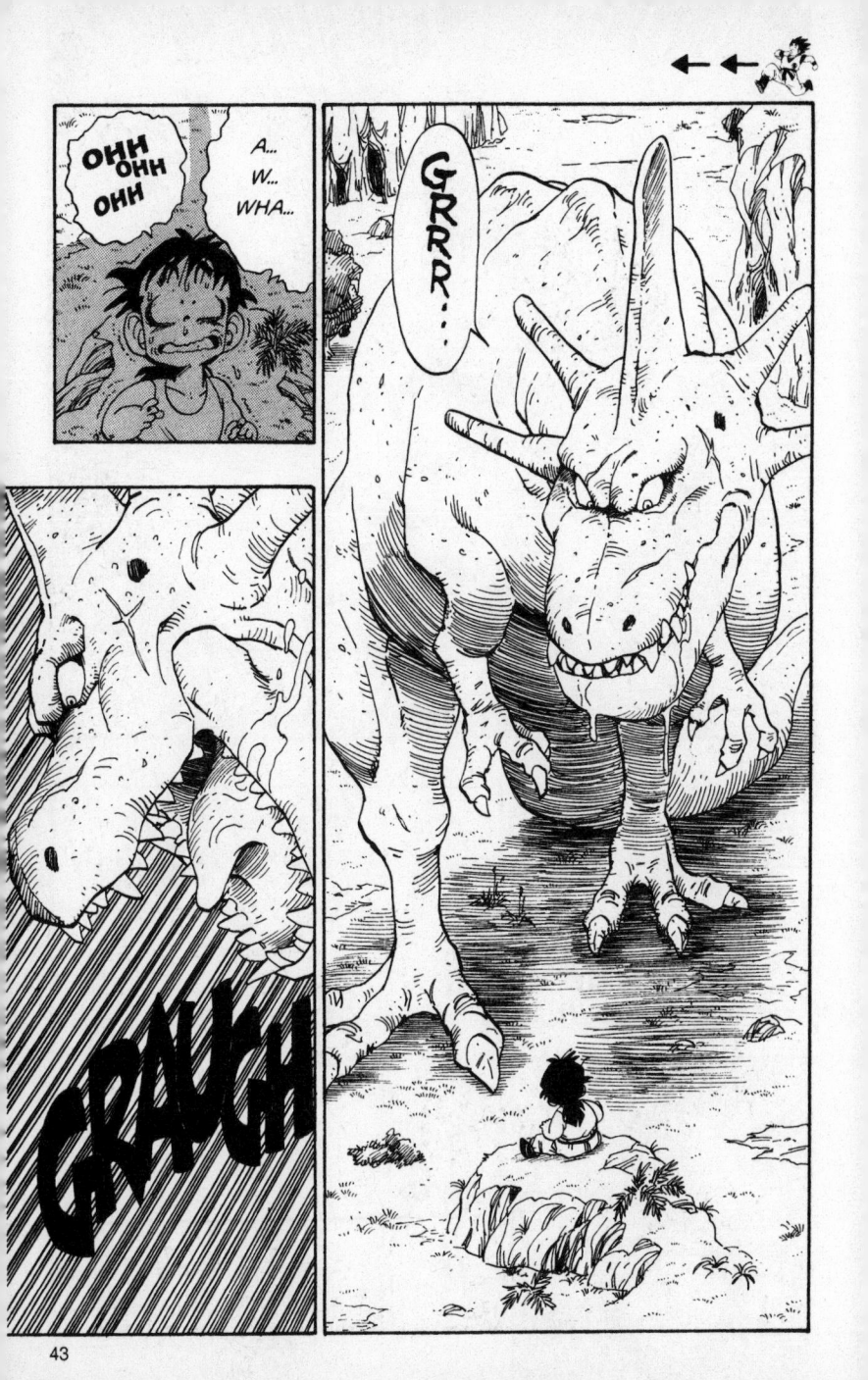
OHH OHH OHH
A... W... WHA...
GRRR...
GRAUGH

WAAH!
SLAP
SLAP

OW!
SRUMP

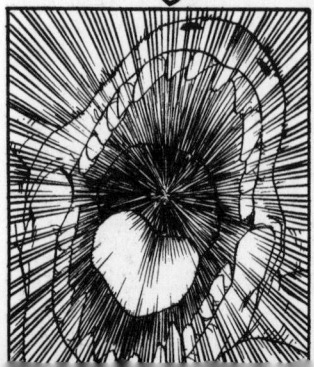

H-
HEEELP!
ANY-
BODY
!

!!

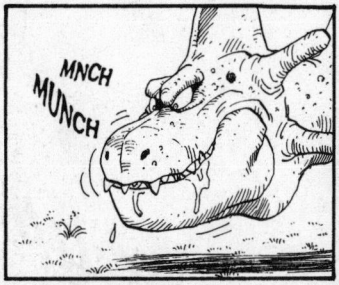
MNCH
MUNCH

!?

?
?

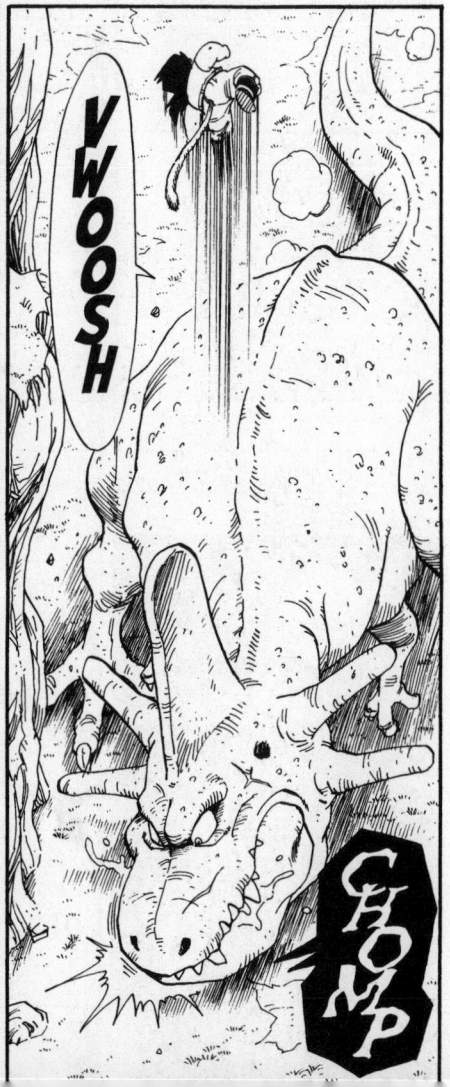
VWOOSH
CHOMP

...?!
HUH ?
WAAH !
I CAN'T GET DOOOWN !
SOB SOB...
HUFF HUFF!
HUFF HUFF!
HWOOOOOO...
GRR
?
?

!?
I'M STAARVIIING... I'M GONNA DIE...
RMBL
I'M HUNGRYYY...
I'M SCAAARED...
THERE'S APPLES HERE !!
APPLES !!
YAAY !
OH !!
?
?
!

IT TASTES BAAAD!
IT'S SOURRR!
MUNCH SHLURP
CRUNCH NIBBLE
CHOMP
MAY AS WELL...
CURSED BRAT...
IS THERE NO END TO IT?
I WANNA EAT DIM-SUM~
MNCH MUNCH MNCH

NEXT: A (VERY) BAD MOON ON THE RISE

DBZ : 14 • Deeds Done by the Full Moon

tinkle
!?
OOF
I CAN'T GET DOWN FROM HERE...
...WHAT SHOULD I DO...?
BUT IF I STAY HERE, I'LL STARVE TO DEATH...
THE NEEDS OF THE BODY...
sniff...
WHY IS THIS HAPPENING TO ME...?

OH !

...WHY IS IT SO BRIGHT WHEN IT'S NIGHT...?
HUH...?

?

...
M...

IT'S THE MOON !
WOW, IT'S ROUND! I'VE NEVER SEEN THE FULL...

BA BUMP
BA BUMP
BA BUMP
BA BUMP
BA BUMP
BA BUMP

BA-BUMP
BA-BUMP
BA-BUMP
BA-BUMP

RATTA
RATTA

...THE HELL ?!
!?

GRAUGH!

AA-R
KLATTA
KLATTA

WHAT ?!
SLIMP
WH-WHAT THE HELL...!!!
GRRR...

WHAM!

S-Z—..MP
...!!

GRAUGH!

BOOM

FASH!
KA-BOOOM
Unh !!!

BOOM
BOOM
WH-WHAT'S GOING ON?!! SUCH DESTRUCTIVE POWER...!
A-AT THIS RATE, THE EARTH WILL BE DESTROYED BEFORE THE SAIYANS ARRIVE...!!
CRASH
!!
ZOOM
DON'T PLAY DUMB... WE SAIYANS CAN EXHIBIT OUR TRUE POWERS WHEN THE MOON INSCRIBES A COMPLETE CIRCLE!

THAT'S IT !!
THE FULL MOON !!
BE GONE-!!!

VWOOSH
...G...
DMP
SHOOP...

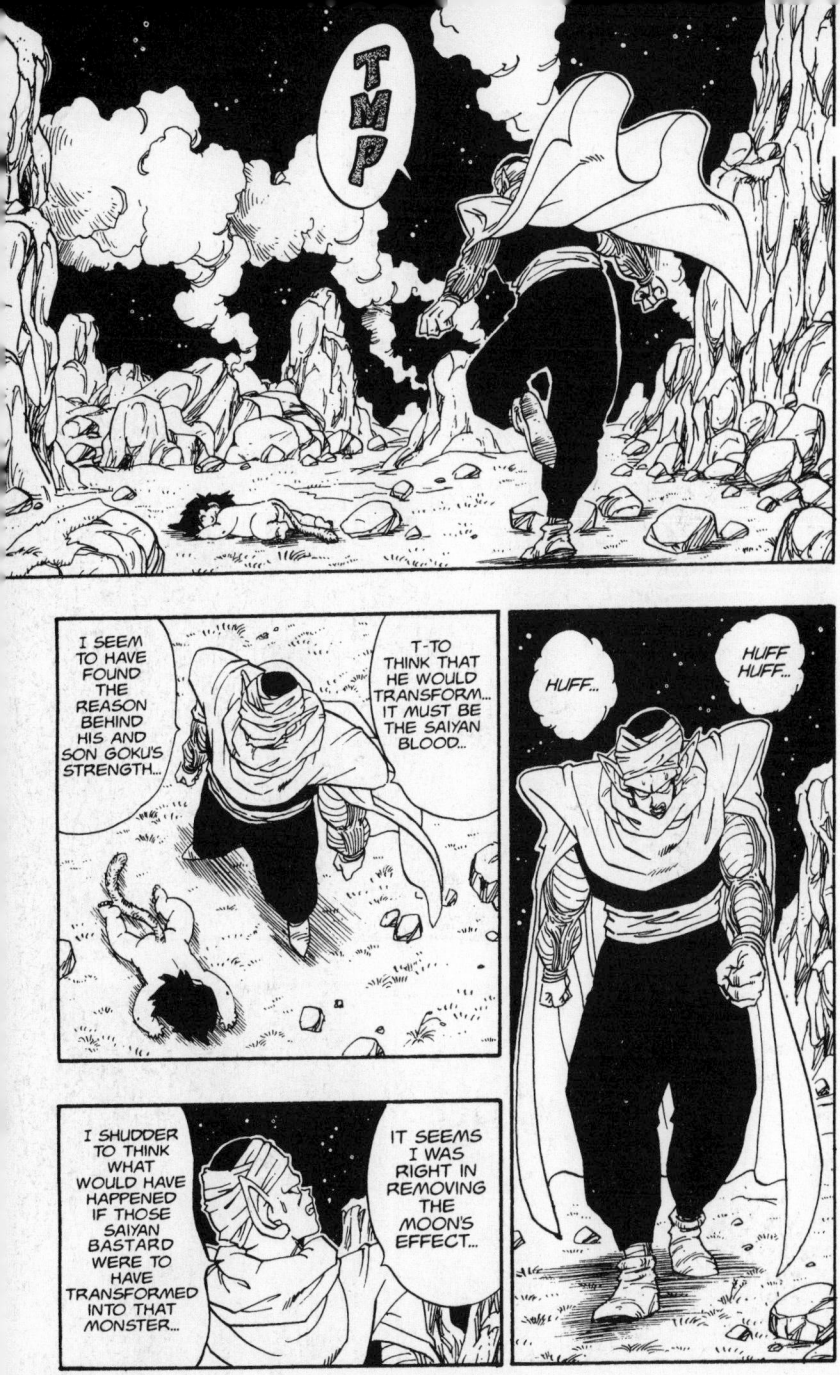
TMP
I SEEM TO HAVE FOUND THE REASON BEHIND HIS AND SON GOKU'S STRENGTH...
T-TO THINK THAT HE WOULD TRANSFORM... IT MUST BE THE SAIYAN BLOOD...
HUFF...
HUFF HUFF...
I SHUDDER TO THINK WHAT WOULD HAVE HAPPENED IF THOSE SAIYAN BASTARD WERE TO HAVE TRANSFORMED INTO THAT MONSTER...
IT SEEMS I WAS RIGHT IN REMOVING THE MOON'S EFFECT...

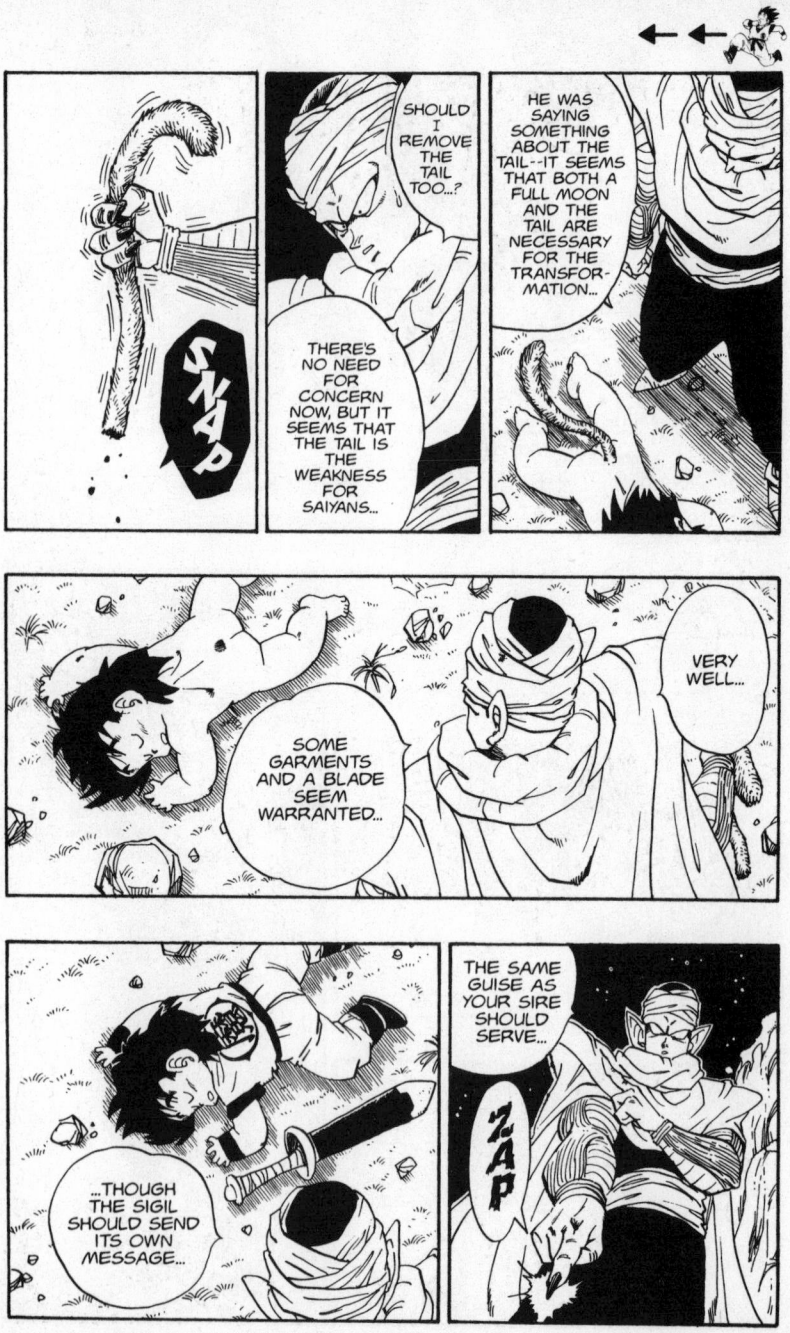
SNAP
SHOULD I REMOVE THE TAIL TOO...?
THERE'S NO NEED FOR CONCERN NOW, BUT IT SEEMS THAT THE TAIL IS THE WEAKNESS FOR SAIYANS...
HE WAS SAYING SOMETHING ABOUT THE TAIL--IT SEEMS THAT BOTH A FULL MOON AND THE TAIL ARE NECESSARY FOR THE TRANSFORMATION...
VERY WELL...
SOME GARMENTS AND A BLADE SEEM WARRANTED...
...THOUGH THE SIGIL SHOULD SEND ITS OWN MESSAGE...
THE SAME GUISE AS YOUR SIRE SHOULD SERVE...
ZAP

NEXT: THE (FINAL?) YEAR OF LIVING DANGEROUSLY...!

DBZ : 15 • Goku and Gohan's Training Begins!!!

KAME HOUSE
CHAK CHAK
CHIK CHIK
YAWWW...
CHAK
CHIK
PI PIPI
!!
HEY !!!
I DID IT !!!
...
SNXX... SNXX...
ZZZ...

BRA-A-A-A-AT!!

...
--THEN NOBODY'S GETTING ANY SLEEP !!!
IF I DON'T GET ANY SLEEP WHILE I'M FIXING THIS THING--

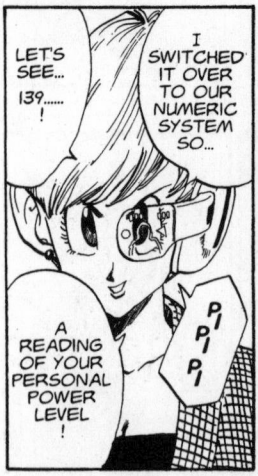
LET'S SEE... 139..... !
I SWITCHED IT OVER TO OUR NUMERIC SYSTEM SO...
PI PI PI
A READING OF YOUR PERSONAL POWER LEVEL !

"T-TURTLE... LOVER"... ?

GET UP !
HEY. YOU. TURTLE LOVER.
CHIK

WHOA-HO-HO!! IT'S 206!!
KURIRIN IS...
SET

WHAT ABOUT MY POWER, BULMA, WHAT ABOUT MINE?!
139...! THAT'S IMPRESSIVE... BUT...BUT HOW DOES IT FIGURE OUT...?

THE BEST THING ABOUT THIS SAIYAN SOUVENIR IS THAT IT SPOTS POWERFUL PEOPLE ALL OVER THE WORLD...AND TELLS YOU RIGHT WHERE THEY ARE!!
PI PIIIIII

ARE YOU SURE THAT THING'S FIXED...?
I COULD KICK YOU AROUND THE BLOCK!
206!

A 177... OVER THERE...
...I'M GUESSING YAMCHA...!!

IT'S TEN-SHINHAN!!!
I KNOW!!

WHO COULD THAT BE?!
HUH?! THERE'S A 250... ABOUT 3000 KM AWAY!
250?!

B-BUT WHO... WHAT...?!
pl!
AND..... A..... 329.....?!!

BUT MY BRAIN SAYS THAT PICCOLO TOOK GOKU'S CHILD AS PART OF A LARGER PLAN TO SAVE THE EARTH...
MY HEART SAYS YES...
SH-SH-SHOULD WE G-GO SAVE HIM?!

OH YEAH !!
IT'S GOT TO BE PIC-COLO...
TH-THEN GOHAN MUST BE THERE TOO...!

HE'S 329... HE'D SLAUGHTER US...
...
ANYWAY, WHAT DO YOU THINK WOULD HAPPEN IF WE DID TRY TO SAVE HIM?

IF WE SPLIT UP, THE OTHER SIX DRAGON BALLS'LL BE A CINCH TO FIND! WE'LL BE ABLE TO BRING GOKU BACK TO LIFE IN NO TIME!!
BUT NOW, THANKS TO THIS, WE'LL BE ABLE TO FIND YAMCHA AND EVERYBODY ELSE!

I SAY, "YO" !!!
YO !!!
CAPSULE

YAJIROBE, IDIOT !!
HEY! YOU'RE THE ONE WHO WAS AT KARIN'S PLACE... UM...ITCHY-ROBE!!
YOU DID THAT ON PURPOSE !!

'SME...

IS THAT A VOICE OR A FALLING LOG...?
KRI

HE SAYS YOU AN' THE YAMCHA GUY... AND TEN-SOMETHIN'...AND CHAOZU...GET OVER THERE NOW!
HE KNOWS WUZZUP.

WHY ?!
EVERY-BODY...AT KARIN'S...?
WHO IS IT?

KARIN DIDN' TELL ME IT WAS GONNA TAKE SO LONG T'FIND YA!
THIS IS A STUPID PLACE FOR A HOUSE !
KARIN...?!

KAMI-SAMA IS GONNA TRAIN US.
ME TOO.

ALL OF US!! RIGHT AWAY !!
WE'LL BE THERE !!

H-HE-HE-WHAT--!?
YEAH. I SAID I DIDN'T WANT TO FIGHT THOSE WHADDYA-CALLEM ALIENS, BUT KARIN...

I DONE WHAT I WAS S'POSE TA.
LATER.

HE SAID DON'T BRING GOKU BACK TO LIFE 'TIL THE BAD GUYS GET HERE.
OH YEAH! ALMOST F'RGOT !

ASK THE OLD WITCH.
HE'S TRAININ' IN HELL.

WHAT ?! B-BUT WHY... ?!

BYOO...

HE'S COMING BACK...?
HUH...?

OH MY, OH MY...
T-TRAINING... IN H-HELL...?!

IT'S NOT HIM...
GYOOO...
NO...

NOT GYÜMAÔ... AND CHI-CHI !!!!?
GAA!!!

MASTER, MASTER, IT'S ME!!!
HOWDY-DOO !!!

OHHHHH... MAMA... !!
HUH...? OH... YEAH. F-FINE...
HOW ARE YOU, MASTER?! IT'S BEEN SO LONG !!

WELL...UM...
A-ACTUALLY... HEH HEH...

WHERE'D GOKU TAKE HIM NOW?
SO WHERE'S MY SON, HMM?

...TAKEN... BY PICCOLO ?!!!

YAMCHA AND TENSHINHAN WERE EASILY FOUND, AND HAVE TOILED EVERY DAY UNDER THE STRICT TRAINING OF KAMI-SAMA...

SIX MONTHS PASS (AND FAST, HUH?)...

ZEEH
ZEEH
AS FOR SON GOKU... HE'S STILL RUNNING... AND RUNNING...AND RUNNING...TOWARD KAIÖ-SAMA, THE "LORD OF WORLDS"...

WELL, HE SEEMS TO BE SURVIVING...!
GOLP GOLP...

AND HOW ABOUT SON GOHAN...?!

HRR
!?

OH, HI.....
YOU DON'T GIVE UP, HUH..... ?

GRAUGH!
JOONG
JOONG

RAAAR !!!
BOING

NYAAA NYAAA !

CHMM
RK
THM
VSHH
OH, BOY!! TIME FOR ANOTHER SLICE!!!
HEY, DON'T LIZARDS' TAILS GROW BACK ?!
GUH...

NEXT: LIKE SON...LIKE FATHER

HYAAAH!!!

BA! GA!
GA!
BA!

TMP

TYAH!!!

SHP
YZZZZ

WH-WHERE DID...?!

HE...
HE DISAPPEARED...!!!

LOOK AROUND YOU!
GNG
WAAH!!!

IT'S NOT FAIR THAT WAY...
MUTTER MUTTER
I DON'T KNOW WHAT YOU MEAN...
IF I CAN'T SEE YOU...
fap fap

JUST... FEEL.
DON'T TRY TO SEE.
YOU WENT TOO FAST...I COULDN'T SEE YOU...!

YOW!!
BACH

PI//

YOU HAVE ONLY SIX MORE MONTHS.
REMEMBER...!

IF YOU HAVE TIME TO COMPLAIN... THEN YOU HAVE TIME TO ACT!!

HUH ?!
PREPARE YOURSELF.
YOU WILL SLEEP, YOU WILL EAT... AND YOU WILL FIGHT WITH ME!

STRONGER THAN ME...
OR BECOME STRONG.
...AND THE SAIYANS WHO COME TO DESTROY US.

B-B-BUT...
...BUT I'LL DIE...
WOBBLE OBBLE

BA!
I'M DYING TO KILL YOU, YOU KNOW!
DO YOU CALL THAT A DEFENSE ?! CONCEN-TRATE !
ACK !
ACK !
BA! BA!

...

huff huff
huff huff

MEANWHILE, GOKU RUNS... AND RUNS... AND RUNS...ALONG THE SERPENT ROAD... UNTIL FINALLY...

H-HOW MUCH LONGER... I-IS THIS R-ROAD GONNA GO ON...?
AT THIS RATE...THE YEAR'LL BE GONE...BEFORE I EVEN SEE THIS LORD OF...
...YEESH... HOW...

ZEEH ZEEH
huff huff

I DID IT!!! I'M HERE !!!
WAAAA!!!
IT'S THE TAIL !!!

!?

...IS NO-WHERE...
...EXCEPT HERE...
...

SOME ROUND THING...
EH ?!
TH-THERE'S GOTTA BE...!
IT CAN'T BE...!

WAHOO !!!!
BOOM
THAT'S IT !!!!
HE MUST BE UP THERE !!!

I KNEW IT!!
A HOUSE !!!

GNNNN
WH-WHAT'S GOING--?!

UH ?!

NGH...! NNGH... !!
HEY! WHAT'S WITH THIS GROUND?!

BO NG
ONNG !!!

L-LIKE... IM BEING PRESSED DOWN... B-BY SOME FORCE...!!
LIKE MY WHOLE B-BODY... IS LEAD...!!

HE'S GOT A...A STRANGE FORM, BUT...
THAT MUST BE... KAIÔ-SAMA?

OH!

G-GREETINGS! I AM SON GOKU!
I SEEK TRAINING FROM YOU!

!!

ZOOP

THIS M-MUST BE THE TRAINING !!
OOKA OOKA
OOKA OOKA
I'D BETTER FOLLOW !!
OOKA OOKA
OOKA OOKA

OOKA OOKA
OOKA OOKA
L-LORD OF WORLDS... WHAT'S WITH THIS GROUND..?
OOKA OOKA... OOKA OOKA...
IT'S SO...SO HARD...!

...HE WAS THE MONKEY.
AND HERE I THOUGHT...
OOKA... OOKA !!
OOKA... OOKA... !

...
HUH ?

HEH HEH HEH HEH...
WH-WH-WHAT...?
WH-WHO...?

ALWAYS SO MANY...
NNNNG... THESE BITES...
...FLIES AROUND ME... HEH HEH...

SCRATCH SCRATCH

OOKA OOKA
TH-THEN WHO'S...?!
WHAT?!
THAT? THAT'S BUBBLES.
...

I AM THE LORD OF WORLDS!

ALL THE FLIES, GET IT? LORD OF THE FLIES?
SAY, YOU STILL HAVEN'T LAUGHED AT MY JOKE!

HEH HEH... I THOUGHT THAT WAS WEIRD...
YOU THOUGHT IT WAS WEIRD!

LET'S TRY ANOTHER ONE! LET'S SEE...
OF COURSE... THAT'S UNDER-STANDABLE...
OH...I GET IT... TOO NERVOUS TO LAUGH, EH?
...
UM... WHAT...?
A...A GOOD WHAT...?
OH, THAT WAS A GOOD ONE!
HEE HEE... SNORT...
YES, I DO.
DO YOU HAVE PIG'S FEET?
WEAR SHOES AND MAYBE NOBODY'LL NOTICE!
I WANT TO BE TRAINED BY YOU!
YEAH!
YOU CAME FOR A REASON, I SUPPOSE...?
.....
THAT'S A GOOD ONE!! WHAT A JOKE!!
BWAA HA HAA!!
THE LORD O' JOKES, THAT'S YOU!!
IF YOU'RE TOO STUPID TO LAUGH AT A GREAT JOKE LIKE THAT...
FORGET IT!
...THERE'S NOTHING I CAN TEACH YOU!!

OKAY, I'LL DO IT...
TRAIN YOU, EH...? HEH HEH HEH...
...IF YOU CAN PASS THE TEST!
SO YOU WILL ?
GUESS YOU'RE JUST A LITTLE SLOW...
...I AM, AREN'T I...?
...HEH.....
...LAUGH AT A JOKE OF YOURS !!
IF YOU CAN MAKE ME, THE WIT OF WORLDS...
I...I DON'T KNOW...
...AND I ONLY LAUGH AT THE MOST SOPHIS-TICATED HUMOR!
IT'S YOUR ONLY HOPE...
B-BUT I'M NO COMEDIAN...!!
HUH ?!
COMIC BOOKS ?!!!
I-I-I DON'T EVEN KNOW WHAT COMEDIANS READ!!
HAVE A NICE RUN HOME!
I THOUGHT SO...

DOOOOM

HOO HOO HOO !!!
TEEEE HEE HEE...

SNORT
PFT

WH-WHAT COMEDIANS READ..
...'COMIC BOOKS'...?

"NOT A COMEDIAN," HE SAYS...!
C-CURSE IT ALL...
HEE *HEE*
I GOTTA REMEMBER THAT ONE.

I MADE YOU LAUGH !!!!
I DID IT !!!!

WHY DIDN'T YOU SAY SO?
OH, MARTIAL ARTS.

HUMOR...? WHO WANTS HUMOR?! I WANT MARTIAL ARTS LESSONS !
YOU SHALL BE A MASTER OF HUMOR!
IT IS SO! I SHALL TRAIN YOU!

NEXT: THE HARDEST TIME OF HIS DEATH!

DBZ : 17 • The Hardest Time of His Death

ONLY 158 DAYS...?
WAIT...
THAT'S AMAZING!! HOW--
WOW!
HMM... WE'VE GOT SOME FLYING SAIYANS, ALL RIGHT...
ON A PACE TO REACH EARTH IN... OH, SAY... 158 DAYS...

...IS LIKE A FEW THOUSAND YEARS OF TRAINING ON EARTH.
158 DAYS WITH ME...
BUT... BUT...

IT'LL BE MORE THAN ENOUGH.
OH, DON'T WORRY.

THOSE TWO SAIYANS ARE VERY, VERY STRONG.
...OF COURSE, THAT STILL DOESN'T MEAN YOU'RE GOING TO WIN AGAINST THEM.

WAK!!
STR-STRONGER THAN...?!
MATTER OF FACT, THEY'RE STRONGER THAN ME!

FOR REAL?!

SO TO BEAT THEM, YOU'LL HAVE TO OUTDO ME... AT THE VERY LEAST!
YOU GOT IT.

HEY, BUBBLES!
SHALL WE GET STARTED?

...

YOUR FIRST LESSON IS SIMPLY TO CATCH BUBBLES!
UNTIL YOU CAN OVER-COME THIS GRAVITY...
...THERE'S NO POINT IN ANYTHING ELSE!
OKAY...

OO-OO-OO
OO-OO-OO

DM
DM
STOP!!
UNGH!!
OOP OOP

RRGH!! 'SIMPOSSIBLE !
I-I CAN'T BE THIS HEAVY... !
EEK
OOK

DOOOM
HUFF HUFF

RRRG !

JUST... YOU... WAIT !
OKAY... NGH... YOU!

HYAARH !!
DM DM DM

NOW I'LL GET YOU!!
GEH HEH HEH... !!

I'LL CATCH YOU... !!
NKH!! NKH!!

EXTRA WEIGHTS ON HIM ALREADY, EH...?
OH-HO !

VWMM
UH ?!
GOTCH-- !!

EEKA EEKA
OOPA OOPA
NUH... NO...IT CAN'T BE...
GOMP

I HAVEN'T EATEN IN SIX MONTHS, AND I'M STARVING.
W-WAIT... CAN I GET SOME-THING TO EAT...?

...ALTHOUGH YOU'RE THE FIRST HUNGRY DEAD MAN I EVER HEARD OF...
WELL... I GUESS...

HE'S TOO FAST...
I...I DUNNO IF I'LL EVER B-BE ABLE TO...
...OKAY, FINE. GO HOME.

HEY!! HEY!!
GLUMP SHRP... !!
YOU EVER HEAR THE PHRASE, "SLOW DOWN"?!

SAY...DON'T YOU GET BORED ON THIS TINY PLANET...?
AH, FOOLISH YOUTH...

DIDN'T GET A LOT OF ETIQUETTE TRAINING, DID YOU...?
THE TASTE AIN'T MUCH, BUT AT LEAST THERE'S A LOT!
HWOO!! I'M STUFFED !!

...IS DRIVING.
MY LATEST OCCUPATION...

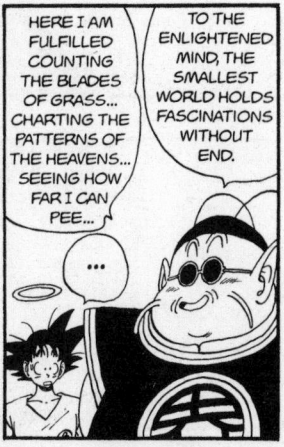
HERE I AM FULFILLED COUNTING THE BLADES OF GRASS... CHARTING THE PATTERNS OF THE HEAVENS... SEEING HOW FAR I CAN PEE...
TO THE ENLIGHTENED MIND, THE SMALLEST WORLD HOLDS FASCINATIONS WITHOUT END.
...

"DRIVING"... RIGHT...

OHHH-KAY... I'LL DO MY BEST...!
OTHERWISE, OUR TRAINING STOPS RIGHT HERE!
NOW GET OUT THERE AND CATCH THE MONKEY.

...I CAN HARDLY EVEN MOVE...!!
B-BUT WITH THOSE ON ME...

HUH ?!
IT'LL BE BETTER EXERCISE THAT WAY.
OH YES, AND PUT THOSE HEAVY CLOTHES AND SHOES BACK ON.

THE HOMEWORLD OF THE SAIYANS HAS GRAVITY AT LEAST AS GREAT AS THIS...
LET ME TELL YOU SOME-THING...

YOU CAN'T EVEN IMAGINE HOW DEADLY THEY ARE...
AND THAT ISN'T EVEN TO MENTION THEIR INBORN FIGHTING INSTINCTS...
DO YOU BEGIN TO SEE WHERE THEY GET THEIR STRENGTH ?

...

EH ?!

SURE I CAN !
I MEAN, I'M SAIYAN, TOO!

OHH...
OWWW...

FEH...
AT LEAST THE LAST SIX MONTHS HAVE TAUGHT YOU NOT TO BE A CRYBABY...
HEH... HEH HEH...

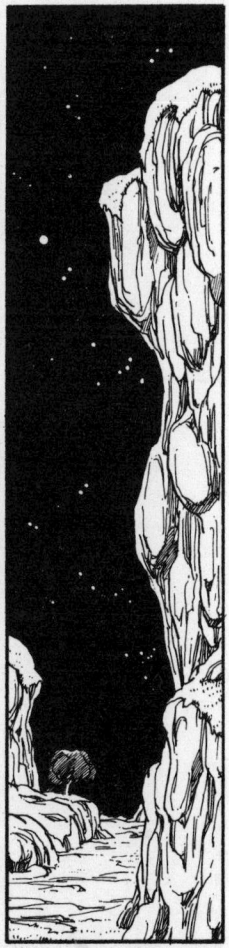

IF WE CAN BEAT THE SAIYANS, IT WILL BE HIS TURN NEXT...
AND I WILL AGAIN...
HEY...YOU FOUGHT MY DADDY BEFORE, DIDN'T YOU?
...BUT MOMMY AND GRANDPA WERE SURE SCARED OF YOU...
I THINK HE'S RIGHT...
HMPH...
...YOU'RE NOT AS BAD OF A BAD GUY AS YOU USED TO BE, BEFORE YOU DIED AND CAME BACK.
BUT DADDY USED TO SAY...
I WILL NOT MAKE TOMORROW... AS EASY AS TODAY!
SHUT UP AND GO TO SLEEP !
Y-YESSIR !
...

ZZ
ZZ
...LITTLE BRAT...!
NRRR!
FOR FORTY DAYS AND FORTY NIGHTS...

GMP
BAM
OH !!
HE REALLY IS AS GREAT AS I'D HOPED...
I FINALLY CAUGHT 'IM !!!!
I DID IT !!!
AND STILL 118 DAYS REMAINING! HE MAY BE THE ONE WHO CAN MASTER THE KAIŌ-KEN... !!!
MAGNIFICENT!

THE KAIŌ-KEN THAT I HAVE YEARNED OF...BUT COULD NEVER MASTER MYSELF...!!!! OH, FOR THAT FINAL ATTACK...!!!!

I'M READY !!!
DO YOU REALLY THINK YOU CAN TAKE IT?!!
SO, YOU THINK YOU'RE READY?! WELL, MY TRAINING IS TOUGHER THAN YOU CAN IMAGINE!!!

I'M READY !!!

LET'S HAVE SOME TEA FIRST...
WOOOM

PHYSICALLY!!! MENTALLY!!! IN EVERY WAY!!!
YOU HAVE TO BE THE BEST!!! THE GREATEST FIGHTER IN THE UNIVERSE!!!

YOU HAVE ALL SURPASSED ME NOW.
THERE IS NOTHING MORE I OR MR. POPO CAN TEACH YOU.
RETURN TO THE LOWER WORLD AND REFINE YOUR SKILLS UNTIL THE FINAL CONFRONTATION.

CAN I TAKE THIS WEIGHTED SHIRT OFF NOW?
YES SIR!

I LEAVE THE FUTURE TO YOU.
神

IT'S NOT ENOUGH!!!
WAM

--YES!!! YOU'RE GAINING CONTROL OF YOUR ENERGY!!!

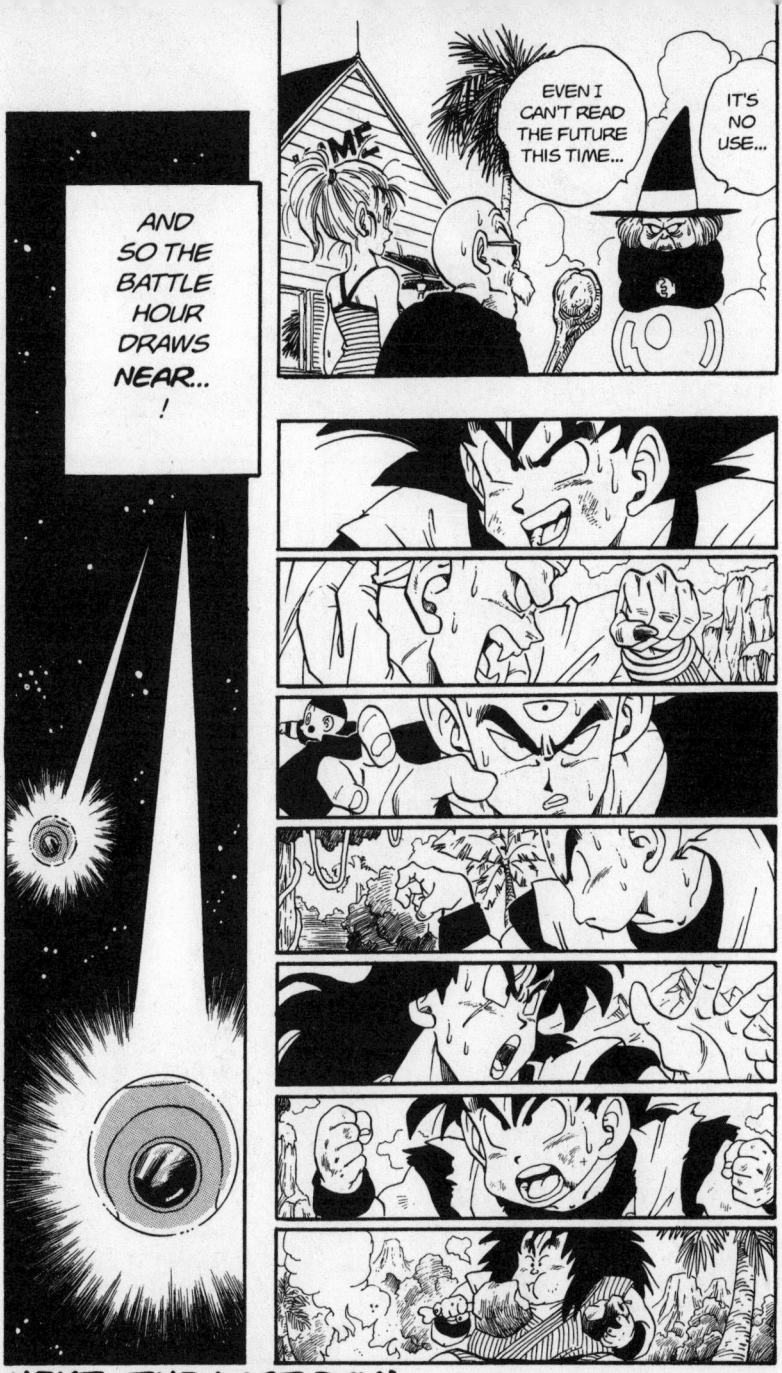

NEXT: THE LAST DAY!

THROUGH THE DEPTHS OF SPACE HURTLES A DEADLY DUO... INEXORABLY... UNSTOPPABLY... TOWARD **EARTH**! WHILE...

DBZ : 18 • Closer...Closer...

CATCH A GIANT BRICK...AT SUPER SPEED!
THEN LET'S BEGIN.
OKAY!

GYOOON

TYAH!!
HUUN

HWSH

SUPER-
SUPER
SPEED
!!!
HAI-
YAAH
!!!!

KIIIIIIIIIIIIIIIN

YA
H
!!

N

SHABOOOM
...HE DID IT...
HE...
SPLENDID, SON GOKU!
I NEVER DARED HOPE YOU'D MASTER THE "GENKI-DAMA" SPIRIT BALL SO QUICKLY!
I WORKED HARD.

IF YOU CAN DRAW SO MUCH DESTRUCTIVE POWER FROM A BALL MADE ON THIS SMALL PLANET...
REMEMBER THAT THE "SPIRIT BALL" IS A MARTIAL-ARTS DISCIPLINE THAT ALLOWS YOU TO BORROW ENERGY FROM GRASS AND TREES, FROM PEOPLE AND ANIMALS, FROM INANIMATE OBJECTS AND THE ATMOSPHERE... AND THEN TO CONCENTRATE THEM AND RELEASE THEM.

WELL. JUST BE CAREFUL. OR YOU MAY DESTROY THE VERY PLANET YOU'RE TRYING TO PROTECT!
...IMAGINE WHAT YOU CAN DO WITH A SPIRIT BALL FORMED ON EARTH! IF YOU CAN ALSO LEARN TO TAP INTO THE ASTOUNDING POWERS OF THE SUN...

THE SAIYANS WILL REACH EARTH TOMORROW, AND...
THE DAY OF THE BATTLE HAS FINALLY COME.

OH !!

NO PROBLEM !
I'LL JUST MAKE DO WITH THE KAIŌ-KEN !

DON'T USE IT IF YOU CAN AVOID IT! I GIVE YOU PERMISSION TO USE IT JUST ONCE, WHEN THERE IS NO ALTERNATIVE.
UNDER-STAND...?

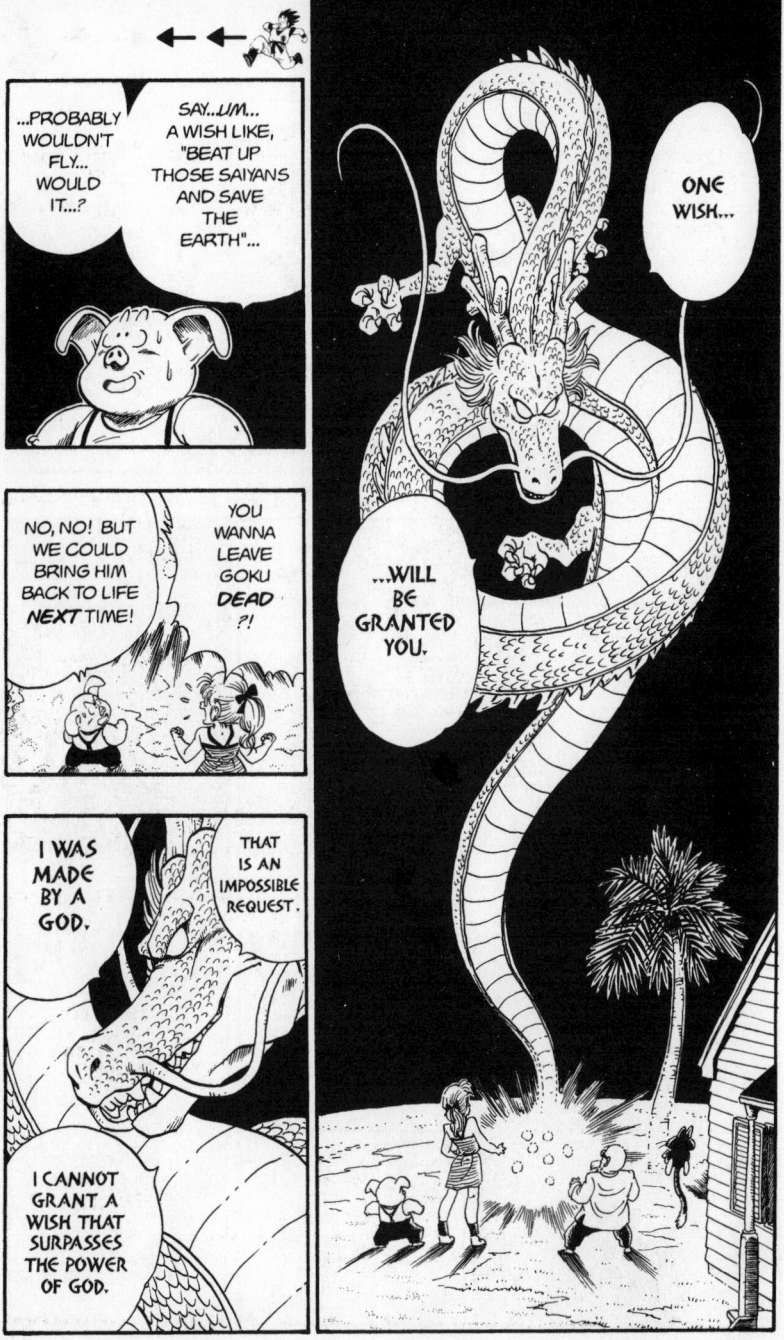
...PROBABLY WOULDN'T FLY... WOULD IT...?
SAY...UM... A WISH LIKE, "BEAT UP THOSE SAIYANS AND SAVE THE EARTH"...
NO, NO! BUT WE COULD BRING HIM BACK TO LIFE NEXT TIME!
YOU WANNA LEAVE GOKU DEAD ?!
I WAS MADE BY A GOD.
THAT IS AN IMPOSSIBLE REQUEST.
I CANNOT GRANT A WISH THAT SURPASSES THE POWER OF GOD.
ONE WISH...
...WILL BE GRANTED YOU.

THAT I MAY GRANT EASILY.

THEN PLEASE BRING SON GOKU BACK TO LIFE.

!!
...BUT IT GOT DARK ALL OF A SUDDEN !
I-IT WAS DAY...

...WHICH MUST MEAN THE SAIYANS COME SOONER THAN WE THOUGHT...

SO... SON GOKU RETURNS TO LIFE AT LAST...

NOW GET GOING !!!
GOOD!! THE HALO IS GONE!! YOU'RE ALIVE AGAIN!!
O-KAY !!!

FT
HEY !!

I KNOW, I KNOW! YOU CAN ONLY COME BACK TO LIFE ONCE! I'LL DO MY BEST!
DON'T START THINKING THAT YOU CAN JUST COME BACK TO LIFE AGAIN!!
REMEMBER, THE ENEMY IS MORE POWERFUL AND EVIL THAN YOU CAN IMAGINE!! YOU MUST ALWAYS BE ON YOUR GUARD!!

G'BYE-EEE !!!

IF I DIE AGAIN, I'LL COME VISIT YOU!
AN' THANKS FOR EVERY-THING.

TOO BAD HIS SENSE OF HUMOR WASN'T ON THE SAME LEVEL... WELL, NEXT TIME...
HIS POWER KNOWS NO BOUNDS...AND YET HIS SOUL IS CLEARER THAN CRYSTAL...I NEVER THOUGHT SUCH A BEING COULD EXIST IN THE CORPOREAL WORLD...

I'M LIKE A LIVING COTTON BAAAALL !!!
POINNNG
WOO-HOO!! I FEEL SO LIGHT !!

THE NEXT DAY, AT 11:43 AM, IT HAPPENED AT LAST...

I'VE GOT TO GO !!!
WELL, NO TIME TO PLAY AROUND !!!

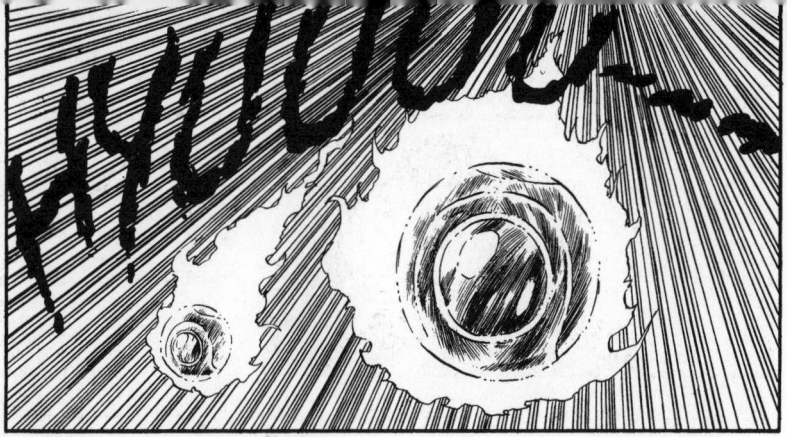

NEXT: COME THE SAIYANS...

IT LOOKS LIKE SOMETHING FELL FROM THE SKY...
WHAT IN THE WORLD...?
MAX
MURMUR MURMUR

WERE THOSE... BOMBS...?
WH-WHAT HAPPENED...?

HERE'S ANOTHER ONE!
THAT ROUND THING...! BUT WHAT...?
Y-YOU'RE RIGHT...!

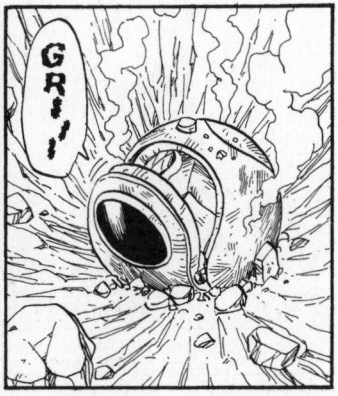
GRI!!

WHEW.

AND HE'S COMING OUT !!
IT'S A MAN !!

!!
!!
MAN... WHAT A HUGE CHI-POWER...!
SO... THEY'VE COME AT LAST...!
...!
!!
!!

THEY CAME SOONER THAN WE THOUGHT...!
CURSE 'EM...
T-TENSHINHAN...!!

WHAT ARE THEY...?!
YADA... YADA
WHO ARE THEY...?

"EARTH," WAS IT...?
PROMISING...

WE SHOULD GREET THE LITTLE INSECTS...

KUNG

NOOM!
WHAT DID THEY DO?!!
WHAT THE--?!
PF

WA HA HA-HA HA!!! A LITTLE TOO WARM A GREETING, EH, VEGETA?!
END IT THERE, NAPPA...
YOU'LL DESTROY THE RESALE VALUE OF THIS DUSTBALL IF YOU KEEP MESSING IT UP.

"DRAGON BALLS."
THE ONE WHO KILLED RADITZ WILL KNOW WHERE THEY ARE.

GOOD POINT!
AND BEFORE WE SELL ANYTHING--WE'RE GOING TO FIND THOSE BALLS THAT'LL GET US A WISH GRANTED!

JUST SEARCH FOR THE HIGHEST POWER READING ON THIS PLANET...
HE'LL HAVE TO BE THE ONE WHO KILLED RADITZ. UNLESS IT'S KAKARROT'S SON...
BEEP

AND IF IT TURNS OUT ONE OF THOSE BALLS WAS AROUND HERE, WE MAY HAVE TO FORGET ABOUT OUR WISH FOR ETERNAL LIFE...
...ALL BECAUSE OF YOUR STUPID GREETING!
UGH! YOU'RE RIGHT! I WASN'T THINKING!

THEY'RE NOT OUR ENEMIES. JUST LOOK FOR THE ONE WITH THE HIGHEST READING...
DON'T WORRY ABOUT IT.
VEGETA...THERE'S SOMETHING STRANGE HERE...! THERE ARE READINGS OVER 1000! MORE THAN ONE OF THEM! BUT HOW, IN A BACKWATER LIKE THIS...?

LET'S GO, NAPPA--AND PAY OUR RESPECTS !
--THERE! TWO HIGH READINGS...! AND CLOSE TO EACH OTHER...

WHOOM
THE GRAVITY'S SO LOW, I FEEL LIKE I'M WEIGHT-LESS!
HO HO HO... THIS IS GREAT !

IS IT TENSHINHAN AND CHAOZU... OR PICCOLO AND GOKU'S KID...?!
THEY'RE HEADIN' STRAIGHT FOR TH' OTHER TWO BIG "CHI" POWERS !!
THEY'RE MOVING... !
!!
THE SAIYAN... THEY'RE COMING! STRAIGHT AT US!!
O-O-OKAY !!
NO, I'M GOING TOO!! I TRAINED HARD FOR THIS!! I DESERVE TO GO!!
--CHAOZU !
YOU STAY BEHIND !

THEY'VE... THEY'VE FINALLY COME...!!
ALL CITIES NEAR THE EARTHQUAKE'S EPICENTER REMAIN INCOMMUNICADO, AS WORRIED FRIENDS AND FAMILY THROUGHOUT...
...REMAIN BAFFLED AT WHAT COULD TRIGGER AN EARTHQUAKE OF SUCH INCREDIBLE MAGNITUDE!
THEY ARE POWERFUL BEYOND OUR COMPREHENSION... WE'D ONLY GET IN THEIR WAY...ALL WE CAN DO FOR THEM...IS PRAY...
I'M AFRAID HE'S RIGHT...
OH, YAMCHA... DON'T GET KILLED...!
TH-THERE'S NOTHING WE CAN DO!!
LET'S GO!! WE CAN LOCATE THEM WITH THIS!!
HOLD ON-- I'M COMING!!
SHA SHA SHA----
WHERE ARE YOU...?!
SON GOKU...

SENSING THE IMPENDING VIOLENCE, THE BIRDS AND ANIMALS OF THE AREA BEGIN TO TAKE FLIGHT...
12:20 P.M...
WE'VE BECOME FAR STRONGER IN THIS ONE YEAR...
THERE'S NO NEED TO BE AFRAID...
Y-YEAH! FAR!
AREN'T THERE S'POSED TO B-BE ONLY T-TWO?!
AND STILL OTHERS... FROM ALL AROUND...!
WHAT?! SOMETHING ELSE AP-PROACHING... FROM OVER THERE...!

HEY.
LONG TIME NO SEE, PICCOLO...
S-SAIYAN ?!
TMP
!
HSSS

OH, GIVE ME A BREAK...
I'VE BEEN TRAINING FOR A YEAR.
TO WATCH THE REAL FIGHTERS ?!
AND WHAT HAVE YOU COME FOR, LITTLE MAN? HEH HEH-HEH...

I'M KURIRIN.
AND YOU'RE LOOKING TOUGHER! LIKE WHEN GOKU WAS A KID!
YOU'RE SMALL BUT YOU'RE STRONG, HUH? MY DAD USED TO TELL ME ABOUT YOU!

I REMEMBER YOU! FROM THE TURTLE GUY'S PLACE...

YOU SHOW SOME SLIGHT IMPROVEMENT, I'LL ADMIT...AND ARE THERE OTHER IDIOTS COMING TOO...?
ALL OF 'EM. I WAS JUST THE CLOSEST.

BUT HE WASN'T NEAR AS BAD AS EVERY-BODY...
HARD...
SO HOW BAD WAS IT, BEING TRAINED BY PICCOLO, OF ALL PEOPLE...?

YOU'RE GOING TO FIGHT WITH US, AREN'T YOU?!
FIGURES HE'D LEAD WITH "SMALL"...JUST BECAUSE HE GREW A LITTLE, THE GRMBLE GRMBLE

THEY'RE HERE !!
THE SMALL TALK IS OVER.

!!

NEXT: THE BIG "CHI"S!

DBZ:20 • Let the Games Begin!

THIS ALSO SERVES AS A TRANS-MITTER.
DIDN'T RADITZ TELL YOU ?
VOICE...?!

!?
LOOKS LIKE IT...NOT SO STRANGE THAT RADITZ WAS BEATEN THEN...
HE'S A NAMEKIAN...

...
R-REALLY, PICCOLO ?
...PICCOLO... Y-YOU'RE AN ALIEN TOO...?! N-NO WONDER...

...NAMEKIAN...?

YOU'RE THE ONE WHO MADE THOSE DRAGON BALLS... AREN'T YOU?!
THEY SAY THESE SLIMY NAMEK GASTROPOD GUYS POSSESS STRANGE POWERS EVEN BEYOND THEIR EXTRAORDINARY FIGHTING ABILITIES... EVEN SORCERY...

BRING ON ALL THE NAMEKIANS YOU CAN FIND! THEY'RE JUST SLUGS TO US!
WHY ELSE WOULD WE BOTHER WITH THIS DUMP?! HAND THEM OVER!
YOU KNOW ABOUT THE DRAGON BALLS...?!
YOU...

ALAS FOR ME, HOWEVER, I DID NOT MAKE THE DRAGON BALLS. MY SPECIALTY... IS COMBAT.
HEH... THANKS TO YOU, I SUDDENLY HAVE A MUCH BETTER INSIGHT INTO MY ANCESTRY...

NOW... WHO IS A SLUG?!
AS YOU WILL SEE.
SHK

SIR...?
I NEVER DREAMED... THAT I WAS AN ALIEN...
I DID WONDER ABOUT THE ANTENNAE, OF COURSE...
神

PERHAPS ONE OF MY ANCESTORS ON THIS PLANET NAMEK HAD ONCE MADE SOMETHING MUCH LIKE THEM...
IT'S ODD...WHEN I FIRST CREATED THE DRAGON BALLS, LONG AGO...I FELT CURIOUSLY NOSTALGIC...SOME SORT OF RACIAL MEMORY, I SUPPOSE...

FOOLS! D'YOU THINK YOU CAN CHALLENGE US WITH POWER LEVELS LIKE THOSE...?!
981...
1220...
1083...
BEEP BEEP BEEP

WHAT?
NAPPA, TAKE OFF YOUR SCOUTER.

THOSE NUMBERS ARE WORTH-LESS.
THESE SLUGS VARY THEIR POWERS TO SUIT THE BATTLE.

SHA
SHA
IF YOU WON'T GIVE US INFORMATION ON THE DRAGON BALLS...WE'LL JUST HAVE TO BEAT IT OUT OF YOU.

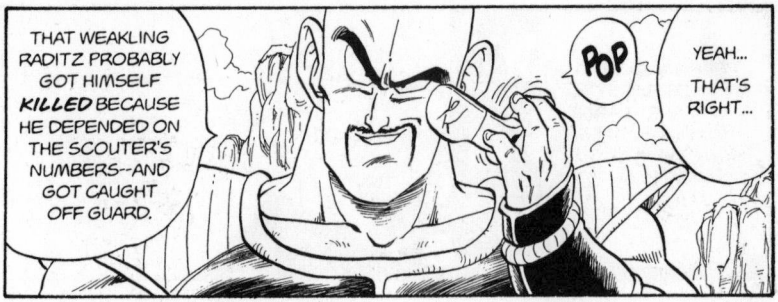
THAT WEAKLING RADITZ PROBABLY GOT HIMSELF *KILLED* BECAUSE HE DEPENDED ON THE SCOUTER'S NUMBERS--AND GOT CAUGHT OFF GUARD.
POP
YEAH... THAT'S RIGHT...

"WEAKLING," HE SAYS...?
HEH HEH...

I-ISN'T RADITZ THE GUY WHO NEARLY CLOBBERED YOU AN' GOKU... *TOGETHER*...?
...

"THAT... WEAKLING..." ?
"THAT..."

HEY NAPPA... WEREN'T THERE SIX SEEDS FOR CULTIVARS LEFT?
WHY DON'T WE SEE WHAT THEY CAN REALLY DO? THEN WE'LL ASK THEM ABOUT THE DRAGON BALLS AGAIN...
HEH HEH HEH.. YOU LIKE TO PLAY GAMES, DON'T YOU, VEGETA.

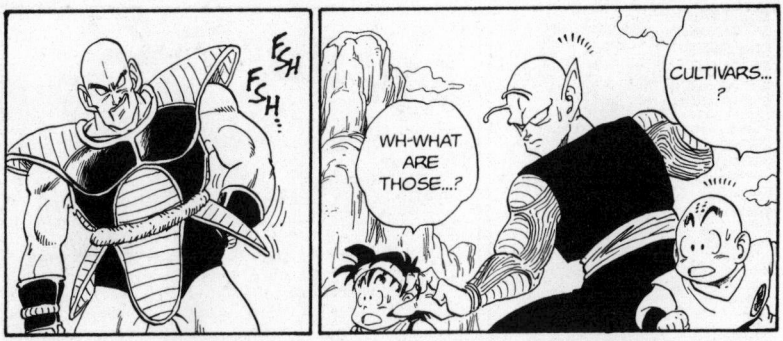
FSH
FSH...
WH-WHAT ARE THOSE...?
CULTIVARS...?

PIP PIP

THEY'LL GROW WELL IN THIS SOIL.
POOSH
POOSH

YEAH, THERE'S SIX, ALL RIGHT.

THERE...
fwip

plip
plip

SHK

SPOP SPOP
SPOP

WH-WHAT'S GOIN' ON...?

!!

SPOPSPOP SPOP...!

GRAUH...

THOSE THREE.
THEY ARE YOUR TARGETS.
YEEE--SH!
I-I DON'T LIKE THE LOOKS O' THOSE GUYS...!

I'D SAY SO...
TH-THIS COULD BE HARDER'N WE THOUGHT...!

!

WHA--?!

TEN-SHINHAN!
AND CHAOZU!
TMP

YAMCHA !

SORRY I'M LATE !

TMP
HUH ?!

LIKE A SWARM OF GNATS...
THEY KEEP COMING, DON'T THEY?

SIX OF THEM... THE SAME NUMBER AS THESE CULTIVARS... HOW PERFECT!
HOW ABOUT IF EACH OF YOU FIGHTS ONE AT A TIME?
FOR SPORT !

WEREN'T THERE SUPPOSED TO BE TWO SAIYANS?
MAYBE YOU SHOULD COM-PLAIN...

QUIT PLAYING AND GET THIS OVER WITH!
A GAME?! ABSURD...!

COME AT ME.
FINE. I'LL GO FIRST.

NO! THIS COULD WORK FOR US!
GOKU'S NOT HERE YET...

YOU TAKE THIS ONE.
T-TEN-SHINHAN! GOOD LUCK!
GIVE HIM EVERY-THING.

I THINK THE CULTIVARS'LL SURPRISE THAT LITTLE MAN! HA HA HA...!
...

HST
GRAWH!
GNNG
HYAH!

BAM
!!
SHHH
P-POP
BLRB
GUHH!
NNK

SSHHH
WAK !!!

HSSS...
SSSSS...
YEEK !!

BLISH

HAAAH !!!

NEXT: THE PRICE OF PRIDE!

DBZ : 21 • One Down...
g... guh... !

IT'S IMPOSSIBLE...! THE CULTIVARS' POWER IS OVER 1200...!
EQUAL TO RADITZ, EVERY ONE OF THEM...!

BUT... !
OUR DATA NEVER SHOWED... !
ERGO, THAT FELLOW'S POWER IS GREATER STILL.

--TENSHINHAN! HE'S GETTING BACK UP!
gruh... !!

PSH

BOOM

!!
BLIGH

WHAT...
WHAT...
?!

IT WOULD'VE BEEN A WASTE OF TIME.
THE EARTHLING ALREADY HAD HIM BEATEN.

V-VEGETA... WHY...
?!

YOUR COMRADE UNDER-ESTIMATED HIS FOE...
DIDN'T I TELL HIM TO GO ALL-OUT...?

DESTROYED... WITH A GESTURE... WHAT *POWER*...!!

OH...
M-M-MAN...

O-OKAY...

LET *ME* DO IT.
I'LL TEACH THEM THAT PLAYTIME'S OVER.

WHO'LL BE NEXT?
THIS TIME--HIT WITH *EVERY-THING*!!

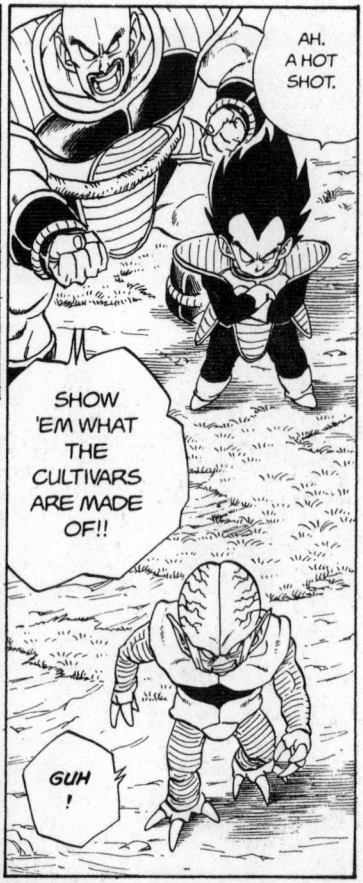

*A STORY TOLD IN THE LATER VOLUMES OF *DRAGON BALL*.

SHIIIII

FT
FT

KAK

THEY'RE GONE !!
THEY--

THEY'RE MOVING AT SUPER SPEED, IDIOT!! FEEL THEIR CHI!!
EVERYONE CAN SEE THEM BUT YOU!

SHHH
SHH
TP
BBBB

GRAW
!!!!
!!
FT
PFF

ZNOO
DM—…M
FNOO

...AGAIN...

I'LL CLEAN UP THE OTHER FOUR BY MYSELF...
THESE MONSTERS AREN'T AS FEARSOME AS THEY LOOK.

TP

!!
GOMP

WHAT ?!

HEH HEH...
SEEMS IT'S YOUR TURN TO UNDER-ESTIMATE...

PK...

HNN...
YAA!!!
KRAK
DUM

IT SELF-DESTRUCTED...
I-IT JUST...
YAMCHA !!
heh
NOW THAT...IS MORE LIKE IT.

...HE'S DEAD...

...

HOW AM I GONNA BREAK THIS...TO PU'AR AND BULMA...?!
H-HE KNEW THIS WAS GOING TO HAPPEN...THAT'S WHY HE WOULDN'T LET *ME* DO IT...

SHUT... YOUR... *MOUTH* !!
.....!

GET BACK, ALL OF YOU!

SETTLING FOR A *DRAW*?!! THIS IS *PATHETIC* !!!
PICK UP YOUR TRASH, LITTLE MAN!

NEXT: PRELUDE to TERROR!

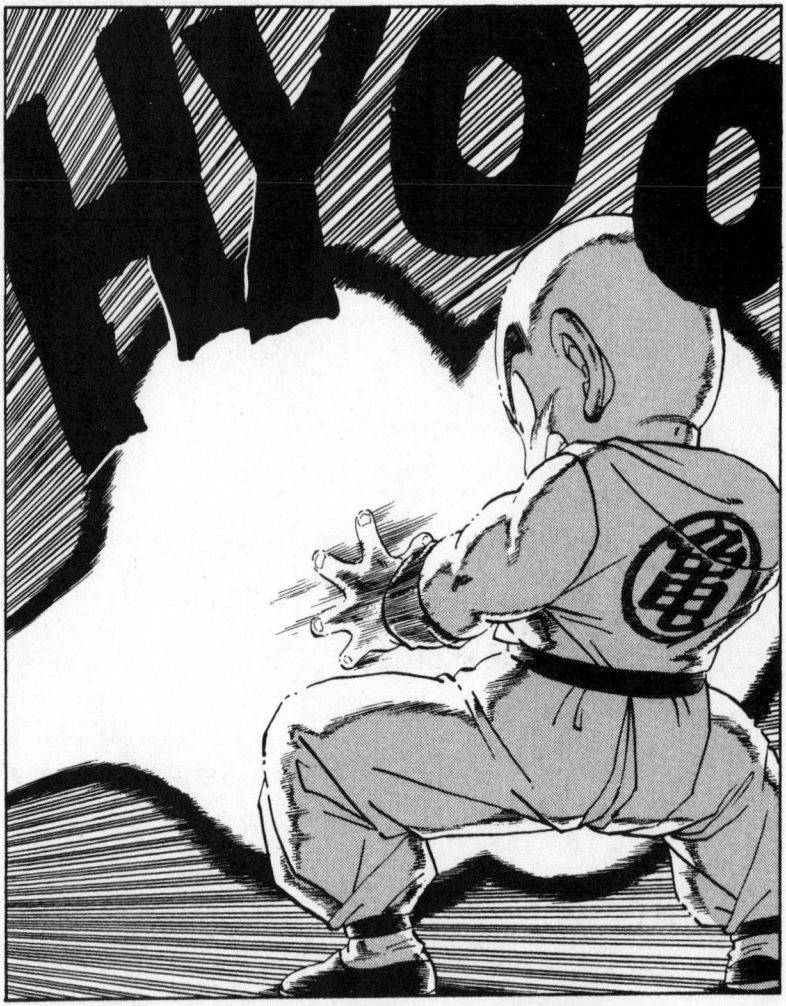
FYOO

!

IT'LL BLOW YOU TO PIECES !!!!
CHAOZU, GET BACK !!!
IT'S LIKE A SIGN SAYING, "GET AWAY"... !!
TREMEN-DOUS POWER-- BUT NO SPEED !!
BA BA BA
heh
WOOOO

GWI
GNN
HYUU
HAA !!!!

BAFF

DOOM
DOOM
DOOM
DOOM

DOOM DOOM
RRMMM...

HEH HEH... I MISSED ONE...
huff huff

HE DID IT !!

WOW, KURIRIN-- !!
WOW...

!!

BWOM

IT'S THE ONE HE MISSED !!!

SHK
DIE !
gg... !!

POF

KNN

GHAAA

ENJOY IT...'TIL HE'S OUR ENEMY AGAIN...
WELL... THAT'S PICCOLO...

HOO BOY...

TH-THANK YOU, PICCOLO...
DON'T MISUNDER-STAND.
I WOULDN'T BOTHER SAVING YOU...

...EXCEPT THAT I NEEDED A LITTLE WARMUP FOR THE GREAT BATTLE TO COME...

ACK...!

ERK...!

!!

I HOPE IT WILL BE A GREAT BATTLE...
HEH HEH HEH...

YOU DID SAY YOU WANTED PLAYTIME TO END, DIDN'T YOU?
HAW HAW... NOW IT'S TIME FOR THE REAL THING.

THEY... THEY MUST HAVE TAKEN IT HEAD-ON...
IT'S NOT POSSIBLE... IT DIDN'T AFFECT THEM AT ALL...!

SO THIS... IS WHAT SAIYANS ARE...!!
B-BUT I... I USED MY FULL POWER... !!!

THANKS FOR LETTING ME HAVE THE FUN...
HEH HEH HEH...

LET ME DO IT. I'LL KILL ALL FIVE AT ONCE.
...AS YOU WILL.

HYA-AAA...
TH... THE EARTH... !!!
...THE EARTH'S SHAKING... !!!
RMMM
NO... IT CAN'T BE... !!!!
MY POWERS DON'T WORK !!!
T-TEN-SHINHAN !!!
I NEVER THOUGHT... IT WOULD BE SO MUCH... !!!!
PICCOLO... HELP... !!!

NEXT: NAPPA GETS NASTY

TITLE PAGE GALLERY

Hi, I'm Son Gohan! I'm 4 years old. When I grow up, I want to be a great scholar.

The Excitement Keeps Going… and Going…

DRAGON BALL

ドラゴンボール

Goku's Last Chance…Is Gohan!!?

STRIVE TO BE NO.1!

Akira Toriyama

鳥山明

BIRD STUDIO

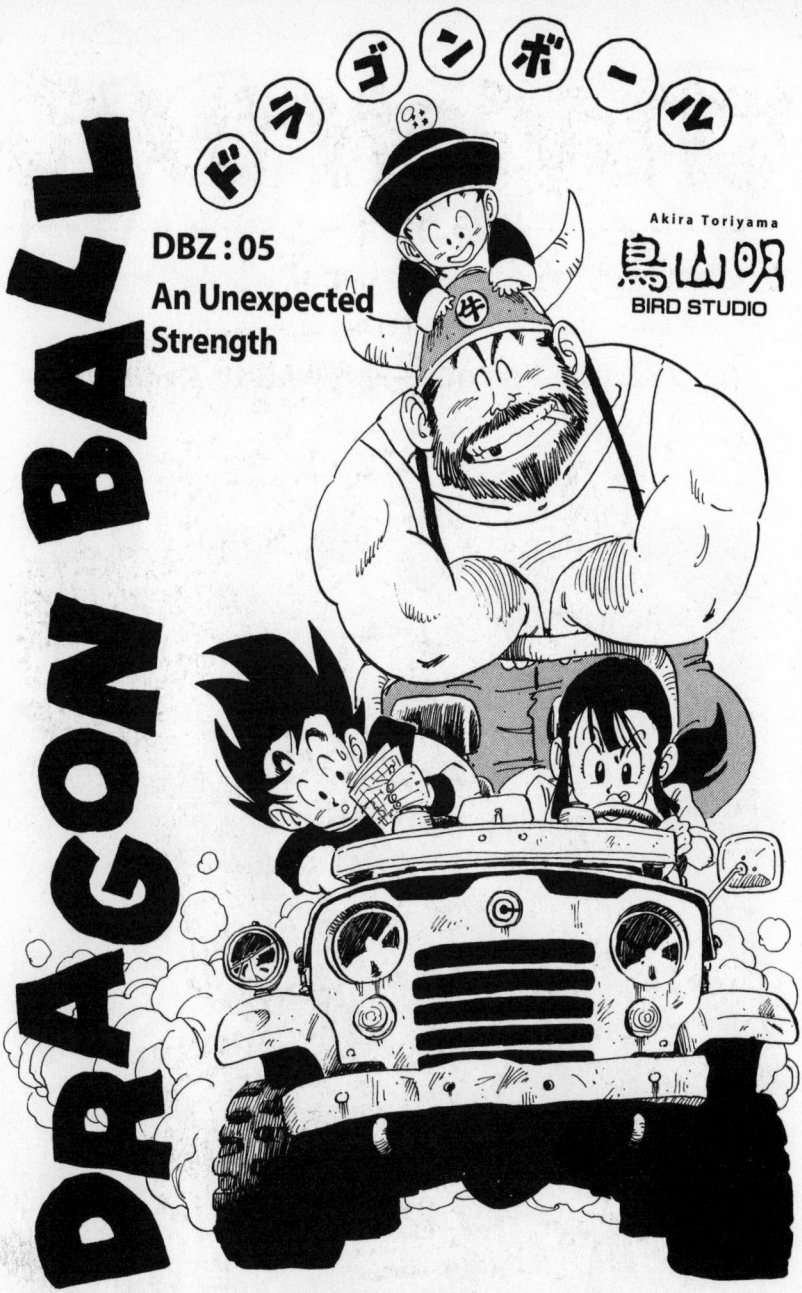

Raditz Gets Radical!

ドラゴンボール
DRAGON BALL
DBZ:07 • Piccolo's Farewell to Arms!?
Can They Pull It Off!?
Akira Toriyama
鳥山明
BIRD STUDIO

DRAGON BALL
Akira Toriyama
鳥山明
BIRD STUDIO
DBZ : 08
A Surprise Appearance
I'LL KILL YOU ALL...
I GUARANTEE IT!!!

DRAGON BALL

ドラゴンボール

DBZ:09 • Sayonara, Goku

Akira Toriyama
鳥山明
BIRD STUDIO

GONE… BUT NOT FORGOTTEN!

DRAGONBALL

Between Two Worlds

Akira Toriyama

鳥山明 BIRD STUDIO

THE FATEFUL YEAR BEGINS

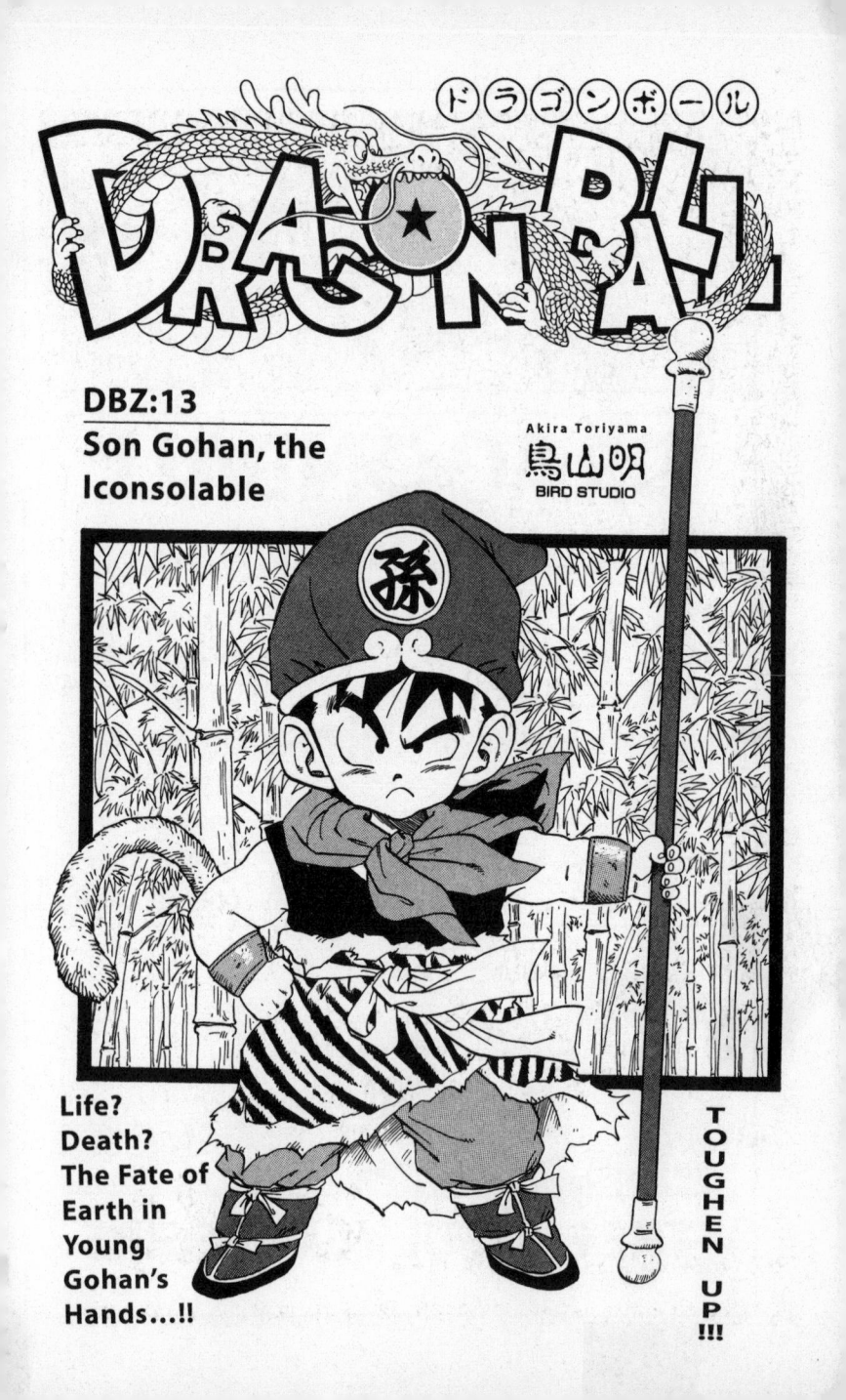
ドラゴンボール
DRAGON BALL
DBZ:13
Son Gohan, the Iconsolable
Akira Toriyama
鳥山明
BIRD STUDIO
孫
Life? Death? The Fate of Earth in Young Gohan's Hands...!!
TOUGHEN UP!!!

DRAGON BALL

Akira Toriyama
鳥山明
BIRD STUDIO

ドラゴンボール

DBZ:14 • Deeds Done by the Full Moon

PICCOLO SHOCKED! THE TRUE NATURE OF GOHAN!!

Train Hard • Get Strong • Go Fast

On Heaven and Earth
Goku and Gohan's Training Begins!!!

TWO GENERATIONS • TWO KINDS OF TRAINING

AKIRA TORIYAMA 鳥山明 BIRD STUDIO

Akira Toriyama
鳥山明
BIRD STUDIO

DBZ:17 • The Hardest Time of His Death

MY TRAINING IS NOTHING TO LAUGH AT!

COWA!

WHO'S GOT THE CURE FOR THE MONSTER FLU?

From AKIRA TORIYAMA, creator of *Dragon Ball*, *Dr. Slump*, and *Sand Land*

MANGA Series ON SALE NOW

SHONEN JUMP
THE WORLD'S MOST POPULAR MANGA

On sale at **www.shonenjump.com**

Also available at your local bookstore and comic store.

COWA! © 1997 by BIRD STUDIO/SHUEISHA Inc.

RATED A FOR ALL AGES
ratings.viz.com

viz media
www.viz.com

hange Your Perspective

om Akira Toriyama,
e creator of *Dr. Slump*,
OWA! and *SandLand*

live Goku's
uest with the
ew VIZBIG
ditions of
ragon Ball and
ragon Ball Z!

ach features:
- Three volumes in one
- Exclusive cover designs
- Color manga pages
- Larger trim size
- Color artwork
- Bonus content

DRAGON BALL
VIZBIG Edition, Volume 1

DRAGON BALL Z
VIZBIG Edition, Volume 1

Get BIG

SHONEN JUMP
THE WORLD'S MOST POPULAR MANGA

大 VIZBIG EDITION

On sale at **www.shonenjump.com**
Also available at your local bookstore and comic store.

RATED A ALL AGES ratings.viz.com
RATED T TEEN ratings.viz.com
viz media www.viz.com

DRAGON BALL © 1984 by BIRD STUDIO/SHUEISHA Inc.